My First Book of the
PLANETS

By Elizabeth Winthrop
Illustrated by John Nez

A GOLDEN BOOK • NEW YORK
Western Publishing Company, Inc., Racine, Wisconsin 53404

Library of Congress Catalog Card Number: 84-72869   ISBN 0-307-02005-3/ISBN 0-307-60238-9 (lib. bdg.)   I J

We live on the earth. The earth is a planet. There are nine planets that travel around the sun. Some planets are hot. Some are cold.

Some planets are much larger than the earth. Some are smaller. Some planets we have known about for thousands of years. One was just discovered in this century.

The sun, the planets, and their moons are all part of a solar system. Our solar system is part of the Milky Way galaxy.

The sun is the center of our solar system and the largest object in it. Our sun is only one of billions of stars in space.

Even though it is very far away, the sun gives us all the warmth and light we need to live on the earth. The sun is about 93 million miles away from the earth.

The planets do not bump into each other because each one follows its own path around the sun. These paths are called orbits.

MARS

MOON

MERCURY   EARTH

SATURN

The earth goes around the sun in its own orbit. It takes the earth 365 days, or one year, to go around the sun once.

As the earth travels around the sun, it is also spinning like a top. It takes one day and one night for the earth to spin around once. During the day, your side of the earth is facing the sun. During the night, your side of the earth is facing away from the sun.

The sun is always shining even though we cannot always see it. When it is night, the sun is shining on the other side of the earth. When it is snowing or raining, the sun is still shining up above the clouds. None of the planets has light of its own. They all get their light from the sun.

Mercury is very hot. It is the closest planet to the sun. Mercury goes around the sun in 88 days.

Venus is about the same size as Earth. Sometimes we can see Venus at night just after the sun has set.

Mars is just beyond Earth. There are craters, canyons, and deserts on the surface of Mars.

Jupiter is the largest planet. All the other planets could fit inside Jupiter.

Saturn is the second largest planet. The rings around Saturn are made of pieces of ice. Some pieces are as big as a house; some are smaller than grains of sand.

It takes Uranus 84 years to go around the sun once.

Neptune was discovered in 1846. It has two moons that revolve around it.

Pluto is the smallest planet. It is very far from the sun. From Pluto, the sun looks like a bright star.

The earth has one moon. It is our nearest neighbor in space. We can sometimes see it when we look up into the clear night sky.

The moon has no light of its own. Light from the sun bounces off the moon's surface.

The moon is made of hard rock like the earth. There is no water or oxygen on the moon. When our astronauts landed on the moon, they had to wear spacesuits so that they could breathe.

When you pick up a pencil and drop it, it falls to the floor. That is because of the gravity on our planet. Gravity is the force that pulls down the pencil. Gravity also holds us down on the surface of the earth.

There is much less gravity on the moon than there is on the earth. A little hop on the earth would be a great jump on the moon.

Jupiter has more gravity than we do on Earth. An astronaut on Jupiter would weigh over 400 pounds. On the sun, the same astronaut would weigh over 4,000 pounds.

We have learned about the planets in our solar system in many different ways. Hundreds of years ago, astronomers watched the skies and made charts of the stars. The first telescope was invented in around 1600. Using a telescope, Galileo was able to see the mountains and valleys on the moon for the first time.

Now we have learned to build spacecraft to teach us more about our solar system. Some of these spacecraft fly past the planets. Others can land on the planets. So far, none of these spacecraft has returned to Earth.

There have been no passengers on these spacecraft, but they carry many complicated instruments. These instruments can measure how hot a planet is. Special cameras on the spacecraft take pictures of the planet and beam them back to Earth as radio signals. Computers on Earth read these signals and turn them into pictures.

Astronomers once thought that Saturn had only a few rings because that was all they could see through their telescopes. But now we know that Saturn has thousands of rings because the spacecraft Voyager 1 and Voyager 2 have sent back pictures of them.

When Viking 1 and Viking 2 landed on Mars, they sent back pictures of flat plains covered with lots of rocks. Voyager 1 discovered a narrow ring around Jupiter. Voyager 2 was launched in 1977, traveling to reach Uranus in 1986 and Neptune in 1989.

MARS

JUPITER

Of all the planets in the solar system, the earth is the most special. We know that if the earth were farther away from the sun, it would be too cold for us to live on. And if the earth were closer to the sun, it would be too hot for us to live on.

The more we learn about our solar system and the worlds beyond it, the more we treasure the earth.